From Egg to Adult
The Life Cycle of Insects

Heinemann
LIBRARY

Richard and Louise Spilsbury

www.heinemann.co.uk/library
Visit our website to find out more information about **Heinemann Library** books.

To order:
☎ Phone 44 (0) 1865 888066
📄 Send a fax to 44 (0) 1865 314091
💻 Visit the Heinemann Bookshop at www.heinemann.co.uk/library to browse our
catalogue and order online.

First published in Great Britain by Heinemann
Library, Halley Court, Jordan Hill, Oxford
OX2 8EJ, part of Harcourt Education Ltd.
Heinemann is a registered trademark of Harcourt
Education Ltd.

Editorial: Nicole Irving and Georga Godwin
Design: Jo Hinton-Malivoire and AMR
Illustrations: David Woodroffe
Picture Research: Maria Joannou and Lizz Eddison
Production: Séverine Ribierre

Originated by Dot Gradations Ltd
Printed in China by Wing King Tong

ISBN 0 431 16864 4
07 06 05 04 03
10 9 8 7 6 5 4 3 2 1

**British Library Cataloguing in Publication
Data**
Spilsbury, Richard & Spilsbury, Louise
From egg to adult: The life cycle of insects
571.8'1157
A full catalogue record for this book is available
from the British Library.

Acknowledgements
The Publishers would like to thank the following
for permission to reproduce photographs:
Ardea/Elizabeth S. Burgess p. **12**; Ardea/I. R.
Beames p. **5**; Ardea/John Mason p. **10**;
Ardea/Pascal Goetgheluck p. **13**; Ardea/Pat Morris
p. **14**; Ardea/Steve Hopkin pp. **8, 21**; Bruce
Coelman/Joe McDonald p. **11**; FLPA/B. Borrell
p. **19**; FLPA/G. E. Hyde p. **17**; FLPA/J. van
Arkel/Foto Natura p. **24** (bottom); FLPA/Jeremy
Early p. **18** (left); FLPA/Minden Pictures p. **26**;
FLPA/T. S. Zylva p. **24** (top); NHPA/A.N.T. p. **4**;
NHPA/G. I. Bernard p. **6**; NHPA/G. J. Cambridge
p. **22**; NHPA/Stephen Dalton pp. **18** (right),
20; Oxford Scientific Films/Davis Shale/SAL p. **15**;
Oxford Scientific Films/Richard Davies p. **25**;
Oxford Scientific Films/Roland Mayr p. **16**; Oxford
Scientific Films p. **7**.

Cover photograph of the emperor dragonfly,
reproduced with permission of FLPA.

The Publishers would like to thank Colin Fountain
for his assistance in the preparation of this book.

Contents

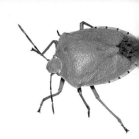

Look but don't touch: many insects are delicate and may sting or bite. If you see one in the wild, do not approach too close. Look at it but do not touch it!

Any words appearing in bold, **like this**, are explained in the Glossary.

What is an insect?

Insects are small animals such as flies and ants. They are **invertebrates**, which means they do not have a backbone or other bones inside their bodies to protect and support them. Instead, insects have tough skin called an **exoskeleton** that covers and supports their soft bodies.

A world of insects

There are over 900,000 **species** of insect known on Earth. All plants and all other animals only make up 550,000 species put together!

Body matters

An adult insect's body is made up of three main sections – a head, a thorax and an abdomen. Its head has eyes and **antennae** for sensing the world around it, and a mouth for eating. Its thorax has six legs and may also have two pairs of wings. Its abdomen contains parts for breathing, **digesting** food and for **reproducing**.

This German wasp has six legs and three body sections like other adult insects.

head

thorax

abdomen

4

Breaking out

Insect embryos grow inside their eggs until they are ready to hatch. Some insect eggs hatch soon after they are laid – some mosquito eggs hatch within a few hours. Other eggs take much longer – some stick insect eggs have tough shells to protect the embryos inside for up to two years as they slowly develop.

Odd ones out?

Some baby insects seem to come straight out of their mothers, not from eggs. A female hissing cockroach's eggs actually hatch as they are being laid, so the nymphs look as if they are being born 'live'.

The baby insects that hatch from eggs are called **larvae** or **nymphs**, depending on the type of insect. They wriggle and break open their egg, often eating the chorion (shell) as they go. This provides a first meal.

These butterfly larvae hatch together because their eggs were laid in the same place at the same time.

Who looks after baby insects?

When a young insect comes out of its egg, it is tiny and alone. Most young insects never even see their parents, let alone get any help or protection from them.

Once insect parents have produced eggs, their task – to **reproduce** – is complete. A few, such as mayflies, die, exhausted and unable to feed. Others such as houseflies leave their eggs and fly off, to reproduce elsewhere.

Different looks

Most young insects look different to their parents. Some, such as butterfly or moth larvae look totally different from their parents. Others, such as grasshopper or springtail **nymphs**, look more like tiny versions of their parents.

Caring parents

Some insect **females**, such as earwigs, look after their young, but very few **males** do. Both male and female burying beetles care for their **larvae**, providing food and defending them from **predators** – animals that want to eat them.

Female earwigs have jaw-like pincers on their abdomen. They use this weapon to defend their larvae from danger until the larvae grow pincers of their own.

Dangerous start

Larvae and nymphs are usually only a few millimetres long when they **hatch**. They have no wings and their legs are often short, so they cannot move very fast. This means it is easy for predators such as birds, frogs and fish to catch them.

Newly hatched young insects have different ways of keeping out of sight of predators. Many are **camouflaged** – they are the same colour or pattern as the places where they live. For example, cabbage white larvae are green to match the leaves their parents laid their eggs on. Others keep out of sight in other ways. Mosquito larvae hatch underwater and float at the surface, breathing air through tubes like snorkels. They dive to darker water below if danger approaches.

A female monarch butterfly lays about 700 eggs in her life. Of these, only about 100 will survive to become adults. For most insects, even fewer young will make it from egg to adult.

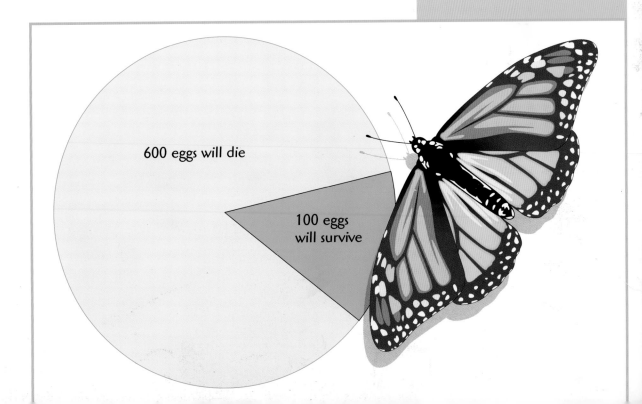

600 eggs will die

100 eggs will survive

Life in a nest

Some types of insects almost always live in big groups in one nest. Bees, wasps, ants and termites are called **social insects**. Hundreds of thousands may live together in a nest that they build. Not all social insects in one nest look the same or do the same things. They all work together to look after the group's young.

Baby social insects such as these bee larvae are fed and protected by many bee adults in the safety of their nest.

In each social insect nest, one **queen** generally lays all the eggs. Most of her eggs hatch into females that cannot reproduce. Groups of these females – called workers – look after the queen's eggs or fetch food for the larvae, the queen and other workers. Some workers are called soldiers. Ant soldiers have large jaws to defend the nest and the ants inside from predators. At certain times of year, a few of the queen's eggs hatch into winged insects whose job is to reproduce. Winged males – called drones in bees – fly from the nest chasing new queens. After they have **mated**, the queens start new nests but the drones die.

How do baby insects grow bigger?

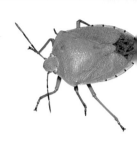

Insects grow differently to people. As we gradually get bigger, our skeletons inside get bigger too. An insect's rigid **exoskeleton** does not grow – so how do insects' insides grow bigger?

A young insect sheds (splits and takes off) its exoskeleton when it is too tight around the growing body inside. This is called **moulting**. A new soft exoskeleton is waiting under the old one. The insect puffs up its body with air and the new, bigger exoskeleton hardens. Most insect **larvae** moult about 5 times before they become adults, but some, such as mayflies, may moult 45 times.

Ways of growing

Different insect **species** grow up in different ways. Most young insects grow wings as they change into adults, but there are other changes as well, called **metamorphosis**. A few species, such as silverfish, change very little as they grow and never have wings.

Just as children outgrow their clothes, insects, such as this cicada, outgrow their exoskeletons!

Two sorts of metamorphosis

Some young insects, such as grasshoppers, **hatch** as **nymphs** that look a bit like the adults but with no wings. After each moult they gradually grow wings. After the final moult they become adults that can fly and **reproduce**. This is called incomplete metamorphosis.

Out of the water

Damselfly nymphs live in water and breathe using gills (body parts used for breathing underwater). Before the final moult, they crawl out of the water – up plants – and metamorphose into winged, air-breathing adults.

Complete metamorphosis happens in most insects, including moths, beetles and flies. They have four separate, very different life stages – egg, larva, **pupa** and adult. Larvae – often called caterpillars, grubs or maggots – have very tiny legs or none at all. When a larva is fully grown, its exoskeleton splits to reveal a pupa. A pupa is like a sealed case. The larva transforms into an adult insect inside this case. When the adult emerges, it waits for its wings to unfold and for its exoskeleton to harden.

This butterfly pupa has transformed into an adult that emerges after several weeks.

Speed of growth

Insect larvae grow very quickly when they can find enough food to eat. A monarch butterfly caterpillar may increase in weight by 2000 times in two weeks. Big larvae usually metamorphose into bigger adults, but this also depends on the size and fitness of their parents.

Larvae such as this rhinoceros beetle go into a deep sleep called hibernation to survive cold times.

The speed of metamorphosis varies with how hot it is. Insects that live in hot places may metamorphose in a few weeks. Metamorphosis may take longer for insects that live in places with cold winters. Rove beetles may spend winter as larvae, often protected from the cold by burrowing underground. In spring, when it is warmer, they leave their shelter to complete their metamorphosis. Larvae that are big enough transform into pupae during winter and emerge as adults in spring.

How do insects get food?

Different insects have different shaped mouths for eating different food.

Some insects are chewers. Like all insects, their mouths have no teeth inside. Instead they are shaped like jagged scissors that move from side to side. Some, such as termites, chew plants, but others such as praying mantids are carnivores – they chew and eat other animals.

Other insects are suckers – their mouths are shaped like straws. Shield bugs stick their mouths into plant stems to drink sweet **sap**. Mosquitoes stick their sharp mouths into animals to drink blood. They make a special chemical in their **saliva** that stops the blood **clotting** so they can suck more.

*Adult butterflies have a fragile, coiled **proboscis** that they straighten out like a party blower to suck up flower nectar.*

Spongers

Some flies have special mouths with a sponge-like lower lip. They vomit saliva and stomach juices on to food to dissolve it and then sponge up the liquid.

Types of food

Insects eat a wide range of food from plants to animals, living or dead. Some feed on anything, but others can feed only on a particular food. For example, the Darwin's hawk-moth of Madagascar has a proboscis about 30 cm long that it uses to feed only on **nectar** from particular orchids with long flowers. Many young insects eat different food from adults. For example, lacewing adults drink sap, but their **larvae** eat aphids and leafhoppers.

Many insects are scavengers – they eat animals they find that are dead. Burying beetles dig under dead animals to bury them and then eat the flesh. Some insects eat dung (poo). Dung beetles roll balls of dung into burrows. Adults and larvae then eat up the waste – and by doing so help to keep the Earth clean.

Swarms of locusts eat any type of plant they come across.

Getting food

Insects have various tricks to make sure they catch food. Some, such as ants, poison their **prey** to knock them out. Others make special traps. Ant-lion larvae make pits in sand 3 cm across and hide at the bottom. Ants that walk by fall down the sloping sides and are trapped in the ant-lion's massive jaws. Some caddis fly larvae spin silk nets underwater to catch swimming prey. A few species of ants are farmers – they look after herds of aphids because the aphids make a sweet fluid called honeydew that the ants like to eat.

Using senses

Insects use various **senses** for finding food. Most insects have eyes made up of thousands of individual **lenses** that can detect movement all around them. Blood-sucking midges find people to attack by using their **antennae** to smell sweat. Butterflies taste plants with their feet!

A praying mantis can twist its head almost a full circle on its neck to spot prey.

How do insects grow up safely?

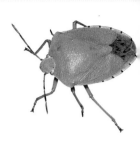

Insects are a favourite food of many animals, including anteaters, bats, frogs, spiders and shrews, as well as other insects and plants such as Venus flytraps. Insects use different ways of avoiding being eaten so they can grow up safely.

The right appearance

Many insects avoid **predators** by how they look. Some are **camouflaged** – they are a similar shape and colour to the background they live on or in. Stick insects are long and thin and look like twigs. Flower mantids have bright colours and a frilly abdomen to look like petals. Other insects even look like bird droppings or thorns.

Some insects use colour differently – they are brightly coloured so they will be noticed. The bold red and black patterns on burnet moths and ladybirds warn predators they should not eat these **prey** because they taste bad.

The elephant hawk-moth caterpillar sucks in air and puffs up the skin behind its head to look like a snake if danger approaches.

Weapons

Many insects are equipped with weapons to fight back if predators come near. Female wasps, bees and some ants have stings. These are sharp, arrow-shaped tubes at the end of their abdomen, which are connected to sacs of venom (poisonous chemicals). They plunge the sting into other animals and inject their venom.

Cheats

Yellow and black bands on the abdomen of a wasp or bee warn predators about its harmful sting. Harmless hoverflies and moths cheat predators because they have similar stripes – they copy wasps without actually having stings.

Other insects have different ways of delivering a nasty surprise. Wood ants spray **acid** and bombardier beetles spray an irritating gas at predators. Saddleback and puss caterpillars are covered with thin, hair-like spines that break off and irritate the skin of predators. Monarch caterpillars eat poisonous milkweed leaves. Its poison does not affect them but makes their bodies taste bad to predators.

The beefly (left) has no sting, but it looks a bit like the bumblebee (right), which does!

Getting away

Most insects see predators coming, but they may also sense danger using tiny hairs on their bodies. When a predator approaches there are tiny changes in movements of air. They can feel these movements through the hairs. Insects react rapidly and escape. Houseflies fly away, beating their wings 20,000 times a minute. Grasshoppers jump away using strong, long back legs. Fleas can jump distances 200 times longer than their body length using **energy** stored in special muscles.

Out of sight

Many insects are small enough to be able to hide pretty well. Some, such as moths and bed bugs are nocturnal (they only come out at night when they cannot be seen by so many predators). Some insects shelter in particular places to avoid predators. For example, fleas hide amongst **mammal** hair instead of on open skin. Termites and other **social insects** make tough nests to hide their groups.

*Caddis fly **larvae** make special stone or stick covered tubes to hide in.*

When is an insect grown-up?

An insect is grown-up after it has completed its **metamorphosis**. It has now stopped growing and **moulting** and it is ready to start **breeding**. Once they are grown-up they do not need to eat as much or as often as when they were young. They do not need energy to grow any more.

The entire life cycle of most insects – from egg to adult – usually lasts between two weeks and eight months. It may be much quicker – some aphids take less than a week – but can be much longer. Some beetles that live in wood inside trees may live for 40 years before they complete metamorphosis. Most insects spend a much longer time as eggs, larvae and pupae than they do as adults.

These elm bark beetle larvae are feeding on the wood in which they live.

How do insects have babies?

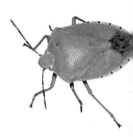

When they are grown-up, insects are ready to **reproduce**. A **female** can usually only reproduce if she can find a **male** to **fertilize** her eggs with his **sperm**.

Keeping other males away

Male insects often compete to get a female to **mate** with. Some males take over an area as their own – called a territory – and try to keep other males out. For example, dragonflies defend stretches of riverbank that have water plants. Males often fight over these territories because they are good places for females to lay eggs in.

This male dung fly defends a cowpat territory from other males because females like to lay their eggs there.

The big flight

Male midges fly together in big swarms to mate. This is called a nuptial flight. Females are more likely to find males in a swarm than if they are alone.

Sensing partners

Insects use **senses** such as hearing, taste and sight to find a **mate**. Male short-horned grasshoppers make a noise by rubbing their back legs against their wings – a bit like moving a bow across the strings on a violin. Cicadas have two flexible patches of **exoskeleton** on their **abdomen**, which they vibrate to make a loud call. The biggest, fittest males usually have the loudest call. More females are attracted to them.

Some insects taste the air. Female luna moths produce a special chemical called a pheromone that attracts males. Males have large, feathery **antennae** that can detect tiny amounts of her pheromone up to 5 miles away.

antennae

The American moon moth is furry to help keep warm at night when it is active.

Amazing light

Some insects put on light displays. Male fireflies and female glow-worms have special chemicals in their abdomens that make bright lights. Each species flashes their lights on and off at night in a slightly different pattern to make sure they attract the right partner.

Courtship

When males have found females, they often move or behave in particular ways to make sure mating actually happens. This is called courtship. Male mosquitoes and mayflies dance in flight. Some mantids stroke each other's antennae and move slowly next to each other until the female is ready to mate. This can be risky for males who may be eaten by the females if they do not make the right moves. Springtail males make a circle of **sperm** parcels – the female then chooses one to fertilize her eggs.

The right timing

Many insects reproduce in particular seasons, usually when the weather is warm and dry, so their eggs have a better chance of **hatching** successfully. These times are called breeding seasons. Breeding seasons can be short in cold places but long in countries where it is warm all year round. Some insects, such as monarch butterflies, travel vast distances to return to the same place to mate each year.

Female insects usually lay eggs where their young can find food easily. The female potter wasp uses her sting to **paralyse** a caterpillar, puts it into her pot-shaped mud nest, and lays eggs on it. When her **larvae** hatch, they eat the still living caterpillar.

Many insects hide their eggs for protection. Female crickets have a long spike called an ovipositor at the end of their abdomen. They use it to lay eggs underground. This stops them getting damaged by frost or being found by **predators**.

ovipositer

How old do insects get?

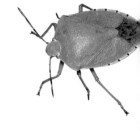

An animal's life expectancy is the length of time it can live. Human life expectancy is about 70 years. Most insects **hatch**, grow up and die in less than a year. Others live for much shorter lengths of time – some fruit flies live for only two weeks. There are a few **species** that live for much longer. For example, **queen** termites may live over 30 years.

Most insects never reach their full life expectancy. They, like other animals, can only survive if they find enough food and water, and avoid disease, **parasites** or **predators**.

Brief adult life

One type of mayfly usually lives for about a year. Almost all this time is spent underwater as a **nymph**. After **moulting** to become a grown-up, it usually lives for just five minutes. In this brief time, it **mates** and then dies.

This larva-like queen termite has a massive abdomen full of eggs. She usually lives a long time because she is protected and fed by other termites in the nest she lives in.

People and insects

People cause the biggest dangers for insects because many insects cause problems for us. Some insects such as mosquitoes and fleas spread diseases among people. They feed on the blood of an infected person or other animal and then pass on the disease when they bite another person. Some, such as locusts or weevils destroy crops (plants people grow to eat). Others, such as warble fly **larvae**, injure or even kill farm animals by eating their flesh. Death-watch beetles or carpenter ants damage wooden buildings and furniture.

To kill problem insects, people have developed powerful chemicals called insecticides or pesticides. Unfortunately, these damage natural **habitats** and other living things.

*Many harmless insects are destroyed when their habitats are destroyed or changed by people. When people cut down **rainforests**, they may be destroying thousands of unknown insect species. This karyatid was discovered in the rainforest in Costa Rica.*

Life cycles

The age that an insect reaches is not important to the survival of its species. The important thing is how many young it produces that survive and have young of their own. This is the cycle of life – from egg to adult to egg. The young are born, grow and produce young themselves before they die. This cycle of life must be completed for each individual insect to contribute to the survival of its species.

Insect maths challenge

Imagine if a male and female housefly mated and laid a batch of 100 eggs and that those eggs in turn developed into adults that laid more batches of eggs and so on for four months. If each egg became an adult that **reproduced**, then within four months one pair of flies could have billions of **descendants**!

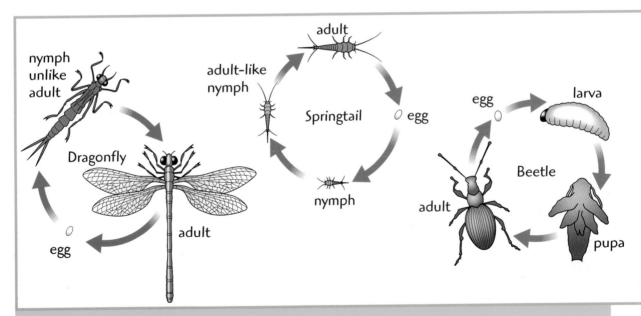

Most insects, such as beetles, change from egg to larva to pupa to adult – this is called complete metamorphosis. Other insects change from egg to nymph to adult, which is called incomplete metamorphosis. In some, such as springtails, the nymphs are similar to adults, but in others, such as dragonflies, they are very different.

Fact file

What is ...

• **the fastest metamorphosis from egg to adult?**
Some aphids take 5 days, some mosquitoes 7 days.

• **the slowest metamorphosis from egg to adult?**
Some wood boring beetles may take over 40 years to become
an adult.

• **the smallest egg?**
The smallest egg is only 0.2 mm long in a fairy fly, a kind of
parasitic wasp.

• **the biggest number of moults in a lifetime?**
Silver fish change their **exoskeletons** 50 times.

• **the smallest number of young produced in one lifetime?**
Louse flies produce an average of 4 babies in their lifetime.

• **the largest number of young produced in one lifetime?**
An African driver ant queen may lay up to 3 million eggs in
a month!

• **the largest wingspan?**
The atlas moth measures 30 cm from wing tip to wing tip.

• **the heaviest insect?**
Adult goliath beetles can weigh up to 100 grammes.

• **the longest and smallest insects?**
Adult walking stick insects can reach 50 cm long. Eight adult
parasitic wasps end-to-end would measure about 1 mm.

Insect classification

Insects that look similar or have similar life cycles are generally grouped together. Grouping – called classification – helps make sense of the massive numbers of different insects on Earth. It also helps us to work out how they might be related to each other. Of the 30 or so main groups – called orders – the most familiar include beetles, butterflies and moths and flies.

Unknown numbers

No one knows exactly how many **species** of insects there are on Earth. Some scientists suggest around 30 million but others suggest about 6 million. More species are discovered each year. You would probably only need a few hours of poking around in a **rainforest** to find an insect unknown to science.

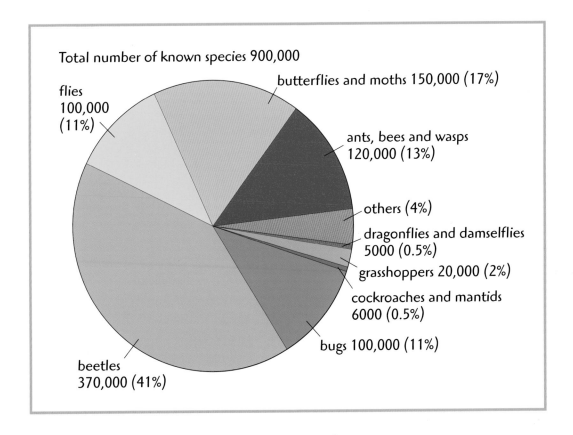

Total number of known species 900,000

flies 100,000 (11%)

butterflies and moths 150,000 (17%)

ants, bees and wasps 120,000 (13%)

others (4%)

dragonflies and damselflies 5000 (0.5%)

grasshoppers 20,000 (2%)

cockroaches and mantids 6000 (0.5%)

bugs 100,000 (11%)

beetles 370,000 (41%)

Glossary

acid liquid that burns skin

antennae pair of feelers on an insect's head used to feel and taste

camouflage colour or pattern that helps an animal blend in with its background

clotting when blood clots it goes thick and hard to make a scab

descendant every living thing is a descendant of its parents and grandparents

digest/digesting break down food into useable nutrients

embryo insect growing inside an egg

energy source of power or strength

exoskeleton hard skin forming a skeleton on the outside of certain animals

female animal that can become a mother when it is grown up

fertilize when an egg joins with a sperm to make an embryo

habitat place where a plant or animal lives. There are many different habitats in the world, such as a pond or a rainforest.

hatch break out of an egg

invertebrate animal without a backbone

larva stage in metamorphosis of some insects between egg and adult

lens part of eye that helps make sight clearer

male animal that can become a father when it is grown up

mammal warm-blooded animal with a backbone. The female gives birth to young and produces milk to feed them.

mating/mate when a male fertilizes a female's eggs. An animal's mate is an animal of the other sex that it can have young with.

metamorphosis change of shape of some types of animals during their life cycle

moulting when insects and other animals regularly shed and replace their skin through their lives

nectar sweet liquid made in flowers to attract insects

nymph stage in metamorphosis of some insects between egg and adult

paralyse make something unable to move

parasite living thing that lives on or in another living thing. A parasite often hurts the thing it lives on or in.

predator animal that hunts or catches other animals to eat them

prey animals that are hunted or caught for food by predators

proboscis tube-like organ used for feeding

pupa stage in metamorphosis of insects between larva and adult

queen largest female in an insect group that lays all the eggs for the group

rainforest thick forests of tall trees that grow in hot sunny places where it rains almost every day

reproduce/reproducing have babies

saliva liquid in an animal's mouth that helps it swallow

sap sweet fluid inside plants

senses hearing, sight, taste, smell and touch used to find out about the world

social insects insects that live in well organized groups that work together

species group of living things that are similar in many ways and can breed to produce healthy offspring (babies)

sperm male animals make sperm to fertilize a female's eggs

yolk part of an egg that is food for the animal that is growing inside

Find out more

Books

The Big Bug Search, Caroline Young (Usborne, 1996)
Wild Guide: Insects, Bob Gibbons (Collins, 1999)
The Wildlife Trust's Guide to Insects, Sandra Doyle and Stuart Carter (New Holland Publishers, 2002)
Handbook: Insects, George McGavin (Dorling Kindersley, 2000)
Eyewitness Guides: Insects, Laurence Mound (Dorling Kindersley, 1990)

Websites

The wonderful world of insects – information about different types of insects and insect records:
http://www.earthlife.net/insects/six.html

Insecta Inspecta – put together by older schoolchildren to find out more about the insects around us:
http://www.insecta-inspecta.com/

Alien empire – information and activities:
http://www.pbs.org/wnet/nature/alienempire/

Enchanted learning – information and printouts:
http://www.enchantedlearning.com/subjects/insects/printouts.shtml

Index